Adobe Oven for Old World Breads

Adobe Oven for Old World Breads

Bread Cook Book

Charel Scheele

Writers Club Press
San Jose New York Lincoln Shanghai

Adobe Oven for Old World Breads
Bread Cook Book

Writers Club Press
an imprint of iUniverse, Inc.

For information address:
iUniverse, Inc.
5220 S. 16th St., Suite 200
Lincoln, NE 68512
www.iuniverse.com

ISBN: 0-595-24342-8

Printed in the United States of America

Contents

Preface

Old Dutch Proverb:

Wie de kruimels niet eerd
Is het brood niet weerd

Translation:

One who doesn't appreciate the crumbs
is not worthy of the bread

Why an adobe mud and brick oven book with bread baking recipes?

Baking in an adobe oven is one small step back in time but a giant leap in taste.

Bread baking in such an oven is one of mankind's oldest occupations. It is so old that we need an instruction book to remind us how to build one and how to bake in it.

This book is written for people who are in search of a perfect loaf of bread. The real bread afficionado who longs for the exceptional and who is addicted to good crusty bread with no hope of ever overcoming his addiction.

Good European style bread has captured the Americans imagination for so long that even the ones who have never visited Europe are longing and searching for old world style breads. With the recent increased interest in artisan bread baking we look with renewed interest to the old fashioned and quaint adobe mud oven of southern Europe. It appears to speak to us about wonderfully aromatic fresh baked bread with a crust, a texture and a flavor we forgot existed. It is hard to make a bad loaf of bread in these ovens, while it is quite hard and a chore to find a loaf of good bread on the supermarket shelves.

Before you leap into constructing an adobe mud and brick oven, please read this whole book through so that you will be familiar with all the instructions. After you know all the steps to take, get started. It will be a messy job, but fun, and in the end you will come out as a winner. I did it and it worked. We were all beginners once. This book has a mission to help you bake better bread. Chances are that you already bake good bread, however, if you have read this so far, chances are that you are interested in improving the breads you make. I hope that this book will help you in your endeavors to make and enjoy delicious and flavorful healthy breads with your family. Good health to you.

Introduction

The pure joy of baking artisan breads in an adobe mud oven is yours with this complete guide to building one and using it to great satisfaction.

Adobe mud ovens are simple to make, last for many years and they are worth every minute you spent puttering around in the mud.

In Italy, Portugal and Spain almost every family in the country side had its own adobe oven while in France, Belgium and especially in the Flanders, an entire village may have shared a large outdoors one. The village oven was presided over by the village baker who was also called the fornarius. The English word furnace comes from the same Latin root "fornus". The village fornarius or oven master would, for a few coins, place into the hot oven the dough that had been brought to him by the village women, and he would keep an eye on it. These large village ovens were fired infrequently. When the time came for the firing, the town crier would announce it, so that the women could get their own dough ready and bring it in for the communal baking. This was especially the custom in the Flanders. There, in bygone years, it was frowned upon for a housewife to enter into a bakers shop to buy bread made by the local baker. The general attitude was that every respected woman regardless of her social standing or age had to know how to knead dough and make bread. At my family's bakery the women that came in would talk and whisper about each other and discuss the virtues and economy of kneading their own dough. They would hold an hand partially in front of their mouths so that we wouldn't hear (or they thought we wouldn't hear) their quoting of a proverb calling the bread from our bakery "the bread of idleness" or "the bread of laziness".This was especially so if the housewife belonged to the working class of people and if her husband worked as a hired laborer. They thought and whispered that she was wastefully or shamefully careless about the welfare of her family by living above her means and heritage. However as the years passed (1920-1950) we sold more and more bread until finally the art of making good homemade bread was almost but forgotten.

In many of the ancient towns of the Flanders they still have streets with names like Fornariustraat - the street of the bake ovens, etc. Some of these streets had several big adobe ovens. Most of them have now disappeared or are in ruins. The cobblestones of the streets are worn smooth by thousands upon thousands of wooden shoes worn by the generations of people who used to bring a neatly towel draped basket with bread dough that the oven master would bake for them. Sometimes the baker would charge them a few pennies, while other times he would accept some of the dough as a payment.

In 1946 I helped an uncle build one of these large village ovens in the town of Axel in the Flanders. There my family had a huge windmill to grind their own flour for use in their two bakeries. It took us a whole month to build the oven and to get it ready. First we had to spend several days hauling the rubble from the old oven to the landfill. Then we used a few more days to get the building material ready. We had a wagon with two horses to haul in several loads of adobe clay, fire-bricks, wood and cement. We worked a whole week building the oven and then, another week to let it slowly cure. This was done by keeping the oven covered with soaking wet flour sacks that had to be sprayed with water at least twice daily so that the adobe would cure slowly without any big cracks. Afterwards the flour sacks were removed and the oven allowed to cure for another week.

Then came the exciting time we all had been waiting for: to start the first fire. We had to be cautious, though, because the first fire was a small one, to warm only, to further dry the oven, and not to heat it. We used a special wood, usually applewood, to build the first fire. This was very important because the first fire was to give a permanent smell and flavor to the fresh adobe and brick inside of the oven that would last for its lifetime. That it is why even up to the present time I never use painted or treated wood, plywood, particle board or cardboard. The chemicals and the glue used to make these items will impart a nasty smell and taste to the oven for its lifetime that will affect anything baked in it.

In 1946 we had to travel 5½ kilometers (about 3½ miles) by horse and wagon to get applewood. In the olden days every adobe oven in Europe had its own peculiarities and imparted its own unique flavor to the bread baked in it. It was the same with the old wooden kneading troughs. The kneading trough was also made out of applewood. It was made clean by being scraped with a wooden scraper. We could never use soap or detergent because such would change the yeasty sour smell and flavor of the dough. As a child it was my duty to clean the bakery on Saturdays. One time I wanted to do an extra good job of cleaning and I used a soft yellow soap to clean the old kneading trough. I had never seen the family so upset. They talked, scolded and acted as if I had given the death stroke to it, because good flavored bread meant their livelihood. To bring the original yeasty smell and flavor back, they made a thin batter out of flour, water and sourdough starter and filled the trough with it. Then they let this stand and ferment for 3 days. Afterwards I had to empty the trough pouring the fermented batter in a big galvanized pail and carry it to the neighbors pigs. The pail was really heavy but I dared not complain unless I wanted to hear another lecture on the importance of never using soap on the kneading trough, the wooden work bench, the bakers peel or the wooden bench scraper so as not to impart a nasty smell and flavor to the dough.

The old kneading trough was seasoned by years and years of successive sourdoughs. When a new one was needed the village cooper was told which particular kind of applewood he should use and how to cure it. They even told him how long to cure the wood. The village cooper usually had his profession as his family name, which in Dutch is De Kuiper. This was from generation after generation. He also served as the lamplighter of the streets lampposts in the evenings.

When the new kneading trough was delivered it was quite a project getting it ready for use. First they rubbed the inside of it with one half of a yellow onion. Then they filled it with a batter made with flour, water and sourdough starter and let this mixture ferment for 72 hours. After the trough was emptied it was set aside in a cool dark place in a basement corner to slowly cure for a week. Then it was ready for use.

The trough was treated and talked about with great respect. It was the bakers family means of making a living. When I remember it I still can get a whiff of it. It had a pungent tangy, yeasty and somewhat sour but pleasant smell that teased the nostrils. It imparted an intriguing flavor to the dough that was left to rise in it. You can imitate this special flavor by using an untreated wooden bowl cured with the same treatment of olden days. First rub the inside of the bowl with a piece of an yellow onion. Fill the bowl with a flour and water batter to which you added one cup of sourdough starter. Mix well and let this mixture stand and ferment in a warm (75º) place for 3 days (72 hours , no short cuts). Empty the bowl and let it dry and cure slowly in a cool dark place for one week. Scrape the bowl clean after each use with a wooden scraper. Never use soap or detergent to clean them. The bowl will impart a good flavor to the dough left to rise in it. Soap and detergent will change that.

The breads we baked in the Flanders in the olden days were crusty, chewy and always a little tart. It never occurred to me that European breads had an outstanding flavor and that they were of very high quality. I also learned that a truly great old world bread can only be produced in an old fashioned adobe mud and brick oven. Nothing else can compare with it. Even if you put a baking tile or brick into your conventional oven, it will not be the same. The baking tile or brick will produce a better crust and it will greatly improve your bread overall, yet the texture, the flavor and the crust will not be the same as of a loaf baked in an adobe oven. The heat delivered to the baking tile or brick in a conventional oven comes only from one direction. The heat delivered in an adobe oven is stored in the thick floor, walls and dome and comes from all directions.

A so called Dutch oven doesn't measure up either. The name Dutch oven is a misnomer from the Boer war of 1899-1902, when British soldiers observed "voortrekkers" (Dutch colonists) in South Africa make bread in a kettle. A Dutch oven is not exactly an oven but it is a portable cast iron kettle or pot with an arched lid and it stands on 3 or 4 legs. This heavy pot is placed right into the coals of the fireplace. To imitate and produce all-around heat some coals are shoveled directly onto the lid. However, the Dutch oven does not impart any special flavors to the bread baked in it, just as the baking tile, brick or metal of a conventional oven will not do it. Only an adobe mud and brick oven will impart a peculiar delicious flavor to the bread baked in it. This flavor will depend on the kind of wood you use to build the template of the dome, and the wood you use for the first firing. Each adobe oven is unique. The most significant requirement for successful baking is getting to know your own. Each oven will have its own hot spots and retain its temperature differently. Adobe oven bread does not only sustain life, it makes it very enjoyable.

NOTE: If applewood is hard to find in your neighborhood, you can use cherry wood which is more abundant in some localities. It also will give a very good flavor to your bread.

Tools and Materials

13 pieces of clean untreated 1" by 4" wood, 21 inches long, to build template.

2 pieces of wood 18½ by 14½ , 1½ thick, to build template.

1 piece 13½ by 12½ inches, 1½ thick, clean untreated wood for door.

7 wheelbarrows full of adobe soil.

1 piece aluminum flashing 3 feet long and 5 inches wide.

½ gallon exterior paint, adobe color.

2 full bags of Portland type cement

1 empty #5 can (46 fl. oz. Juice can)

1 piece of chicken wire 16" by 22"

1 piece of chicken wire 18" by 20"

1 piece of chicken wire 5 feet long by 3 feet wide.

20 fire bricks 2 ½ x 3 ¾ x 7 ¾.

30 concrete blocks 8 x 8 x 16

10 concrete cap blocks 8 x 2 x 16

Shovel

Hammer

Hoe

Power Saw

Saber Saw

Wire Cutter

Tape Measure

Pencils

Rags

Tarp.

Step by Step Directions

If this is the first adobe-mud oven you are going to build, the size described in this book will be just the right one, as it is simple to build and it is very economical on firewood. With just one firing you will be able to bake several times. As an example, you should be able to bake the flat bread (pizza, focaccia, etc,) first, then the regular one, and for last, the sweet dough. However, if you decide to build a bigger oven, all you need to do is to build a larger platform and a larger template. The vent hole and the door opening should stay the same size. Only remember that the larger the oven the more firewood it is required to heat it.

Step One:

Find a level place, a little away from yours and your neighbors house, and away from anything combustible. Check with the local officials about property line setback and with the Fire Department about regulations. Some localities will require a chimney with a spark arrester. If that is the case in your area you can fit a piece of ¼" wire mesh over a #5 can (46 fl. oz. juice can) that has its top and bottom lids cut out. Fasten the mesh well over the top opening so as to arrest any sparks. Even if that is not the law, it is a good safety precaution.

Step Two:

Build a platform or base 40 inches long x 32 wide and 24 inches high with the 30 (8x8x16) concrete blocks, stacking them cris-cross, without mortar, to accommodate future disassembly. Top the platform with the 10 cap (8x2x16) blocks. It should be now 26 inches high. This will be just high enough to prevent you from stooping and bending over when using your oven, thus saving your back

Step Three:

Using a large empty can (large coffee can size) to measure, mix 5 cans

adobe soil with 2 cans Portland cement in a wheelbarrow. Add water and use a hoe to mix the mud to a consistency of a thick porridge or of a mud pie. Slater this mixture on the top of the platform about 1½ inches thick, leveling it very carefully, since you will not have a chance to level the oven floor again. Starting on the outermost front end edge set the 20 (2¼ x 3¾ x 7¾) fire-bricks in 4 rows of 5 each abreast into the leveled mud, leaving a space of 6¾ inches at each side and 9 inches in the back. The bricks should be pressed into the soft mud as close as possible and lev-

eled with each other. This is important because a leveled hearth will be easy to clean with a hoe or shovel later on. You will have now an oven floor of 31 x 18½ inches on top of the 40 x 32 inches platform. The height of the whole structure should be 30 inches.

Note: If your firebricks are of a different size, you will need to make adjustments accordingly.

Step Four:

Use clean, unpainted and untreated, preferably apple or cherry wood, to build a template. Do not use wood that has varnish, glue or any chemicals. Such will give a permanent bad smell to your oven and consequently a bad taste to the bread baked in it. The wooden template will burn out with the first fire. The outermost edge of the template will make the measurement of the baking chamber.

Start out with the 2 pieces of 1½ thick wood, 18½ inches wide and 14½ inches high. Round off the vertical top corners of both pieces, equally, so that the peak of the rounded top is still 14½ inches high. This will make the dome. Connect lengthwise these front and back pieces with the 13 strips of wood 21 inches long 1" x 4" wide, nailing them in place to form a rounded top box 21 inches long. On the 18½ wide piece of wood that will be the back, center toward the top a #5 can, and draw a circle with a pencil, around it. Following the circle, cut out the vent hole that will fit the #5 can that you have set aside for the purpose of a chimney.

The opposite side of the vent hole will be the front part. On this, cut out a 8" x 8" square hole that will be used as an entrance to load the firewood through, later. Now you have your template ready. Set it in place over the firebricks, clear to the outermost back edge, so as to have a more generous hearth up front.

Step Five:

Prepare the chicken wire that you will use later in the adobe mud that will cover the oven so as to prevent cracks in it and help to hold it together. You will need several different sizes. One will be a piece 5 feet long by 3 feet wide. A different piece will be 20 inches by 18 inches where there should be made a round hole in the middle, close to the top, about 4 inches in diameter, to accommodate the #5 can in the vent hole. The third piece of the chicken wire should be 22 inches by 16 inches to be used at the front end of the oven. Leaving 4½ inches on each side of the 22 inches width starting at the bottom cut out a hole 13 inches wide and 12 inches high so as to fit the door.

Step Six:

To make the door of the oven, saw a plank of clean untreated wood that is1½ inches thick to have almost a square, sized 13½ inches wide and 12½ inches high. Round off the top corners so that the peak of the dome is still 12½ inches high. Cut 2 pieces of 2" x 2" wood 12 inches long and attach them cross wise onto the door, about 4 to 5 inches apart. Saw another piece off a 2" x 2" 12 inches long, and fasten it vertically to the center of the cross pieces to serve as a handle.

Step Seven:

Tack the 5 inch aluminum flashing around the outermost edge of the door. Smear some vaseline or petroleum jelly on it, and also on the #5 can that fits in as a flue. This will prevent the adobe mud mixture from sticking to these items, so that you can remove them later. Set the door with the flashing tightly fitted against the front end of the template, and place the can into the back vent hole.

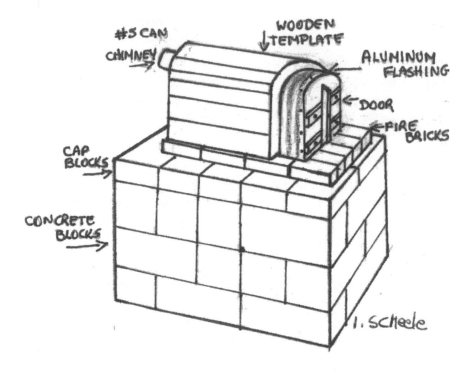

Step Eight:

Using a large empty coffee can to measure, mix with a hoe, 5 cans of adobe soil to 2 cans of Portland style cement, in a wheelbarrow. Add enough water to get the consistency of a thick porridge or mud pie. Working from the bottom of the template on up, pack the mud mixture firmly over the template leaving no air pockets. When the whole template is covered with 2½ to 3 inches press the 5 feet by 3 feet of chicken wire over and into the mud on the top and on the sides. Then press the 18"x20" piece with the round hole over and into the mud of the back centering it

over the flue. Do the same with the 22"x16" front end piece around the door opening. Continue to add the adobe mixture until the coat is seven inches thick all around. Do not skimp. If you have less than 7 inches of mud all around, the oven will have trouble retaining its heat. Make sure that you press the second layer of mud firmly into and over the chicken wire, packing it carefully around the #5 can in the back. With the adobe build a nice arch around the door, smoothing it out with a wet gloved hand that you dip into water often. Wiggle the door and the flue a little to prevent them from sticking. Plaster the four sides of the platform, the base, the whole structure evenly with the leftover mixture.

Cover the oven with wet rags. Twice daily spray them with water to keep them wet. Place a tarp over the rags to prevent them from drying out. Keep them wet and covered for a week to give a chance to the adobe to cure very slowly. After a week remove the wet rags and let the oven cure for another week.

Step Nine:

After a week that the oven has been curing without the covers, very carefully take the door out and remove the metal flashing. Remove the #5 can from the rear vent hole. Let the oven dry out with the door and vent open for another seven days.

Step Ten:

Time for the first fire. There is a need for caution here. The purpose of the first fire is to burn the template and to warm the oven moderately so as to further dry it out. It is not to heat it with a big roaring fire.

With the door and the vent open build and light a small fire using clean and untreated wood, preferably cherry or apple. After the fire has burned down, rake the ashes out with an hoe or shovel, being careful on how to dispose of them, making sure you do not have any live embers. Let the oven completely cool for 24 hours or more.

Step Eleven:

Use some clean kindling wood to start a fire and then add some logs to build an hot fire for 5 to 5½ hours until the outside surface of the oven is quite hot to the touch. Use a poker to rearrange the burning logs. When these have burned down to coals, with an hoe spread these evenly over the whole oven floor, to ensure equal heat. When most of the coals have turned to ashes remove them carefully with an hoe or shovel into a metal pail remembering that there are live embers in it. Pour water in the pail and dispose the wet ashes properly. With a wet cotton string mop clean the hearth. Or if you want to avoid the mopping chore, do as I do. Place a clean 14½ x 16½ heavy duty baking tile onto the oven floor. On the top of the tile place a metal thermometer. Block the flue with wet rags. Soak the door in water and close the oven for 20 minutes. This will heat the tile and it will also bring the oven to the right temperature. Usually an oven will be too hot for baking bread right after you take the ashes out. Heating the heavy duty baking tile for 20 minutes will drop the temperature to the right range.

A baking tile on the brick floor of an adobe oven is very different from one in a conventional oven. In a conventional oven the heat is delivered from one direction. In an adobe oven the heat comes from all directions and the tile becomes part of it. The temperature for baking in an adobe oven is the same as in a conventional one. If you can hold your hand in the middle of the oven and count to 8 it probably is too cool. A metal oven thermometer that reads up to 600° F. or higher will be very useful. If you do not use a baking tile, right after you mop the hearth, set the thermometer on the oven floor inside the baking chamber.

Soak the door in water and close it over the entrance. Block the vent opening. After ten minutes open the door and read the temperature. By following the instructions and recipes in later chapters of this book you may now be ready to load your first loaves in the oven.

Step Twelve:

When the oven is ready, place the loaves onto a baker's peel that has been liberally dusted with cornmeal. This will help the loaves slide off easily. For an old world decorative look , use a sharp razor to make 4 or 5 diagonal slashes about ¼ inch deep across the top of the loaves. Insert the baker's peel into the oven and give it a rapid push-pull action to eject the loaves onto the tile or directly onto the hearth. There will be enough heat stored in the floor, walls and top for it to radiate the entire chamber so it can be used several times. Flat breads should be baked first, then regular white or whole-wheat. Sweet and raisin breads should be baked last. Always place the biggest loaves in the back, smaller loaves up front. The intense and immediate heat will give the dough a final burst of life called the oven spring. The oven spring makes for a light crusty loaf.

Step Thirteen:

After waiting for the time indicated in the recipes, open the oven door and use a baker's peel to remove the hot loaves. If you are baking more than one batch, work quickly to save the heat.

Step Fourteen:

After the oven is heated several times it likely will develop some harmless hairline cracks. Now is the time to paint the oven. The paint will seal the cracks. Use an adobe color latex paint when the oven is cool and wait for it to dry thoroughly before lighting a fire in it again. For a pleasant aesthetic look paint the whole structure, including the base. You may repaint it later a few more times.

Useful Tips

Firewood: I use mostly oak for firewood. However if firewood is expensive and hard to find in your neighborhood you can start a small fire with good wood and then toss in about 5 pounds of charcoal briquettes. Let them burn for about 45 minutes and then add another 5 pounds. Let them burn until the outside of the oven is quite hot to the touch. Use a shovel to remove the hot coals and ashes placing them into a metal bucket. Wet mop the hearth. Proceed as instructions on step eleven.

Using Steam For a Crustier Bread: In Europe, to make crustier breads, a pail with water was placed in the back of the big oven which is the hottest part. For a small oven you can imitate this by filling with water a small coffee can that has a pin-prick hole in the bottom. Place it in the back of the oven. As the water slowly seeps out it will create an abundance of steam. This will create a better oven spring and make for a real crusty bread. If more steam is needed, place a soaking wet towel or rag on the front part of the hearth just before you close the door. The reason for an extra oven spring by using steam, is that it will prevent a crust from forming too quickly keeping the dough elastic a little longer and giving it a little more time to rise. In addition, it will be helpful to brush the loaves with plain water just before baking.

Timing: It is better for the oven to be ready before the dough. As long as you will keep the door and the vent closed the oven will keep its temperature for at least an hour or more. If you see that the dough will be ready before the oven, you can slow down the fermentation by putting the dough into the refrigerator. This will not kill the fermentation but it will slow it down. A good rule of thumb is to shape the dough into loaves and then quickly clean the oven floor. Close the oven and wait for about 20 to 30 minutes, while the dough is rising. Then you can place the loaves into the oven and bake according to the time indicated in the recipes. For the first time bakers, it would be better to experiment with slightly less yeast and a little cooler dough temperature. This will slow the fermentation down and the timing will be easier to control. As a bonus you will notice that the slower process will give your finished product a better flavor. Among European bakers this is known as the Flemish method which is used to improve the flavor, the crust and the texture.

Fermentation: A simple way to improve the flavor and the texture of your bread is to save a piece of dough and use it in the next batch. This saved piece will continue to ferment and develop a very nice flavor. Adding it to the new dough will create a moist and light loaf full of flavor, eliminating the need for fat.

Defining Doneness: To know when the bread has baked long enough, after you take it out of the oven, tap its bottom with your fingers. If the loaf rings hollow, it is done. Otherwise return it to the oven and let it bake another 5 to 10 minutes. Experience is the best teacher, as each oven is different. After you have finished baking for the day, fill the oven with firewood for the next time. The residual heat will help to dry the wood which will be very helpful for the next time you use it. Such drier wood will be easier to light and it will produce a lot of less smoke.

Bakers Peel: This is a long wooden paddle that is very helpful in preventing the burning of your hands or fingers as you load or unload the hot oven. It is not difficult to make your own. Just cut a piece of thin wood or plywood about 10 inches wide and 12 inches long. Shape it like a paddle by rounding off the corners. Smooth it with sand paper and fasten it to a broom handle or to a long stick. A bakers peel is also an instrument that will make it easy to slide the loaves, pizza or other flat breads directly onto the oven hearth.

Appearance: You can shape your loaves by hand so that they are round, oblong, long or flat. To add to the attractiveness of your bread you can slash the top with a sharp knife or razor blade making different designs. You can also use a generously floured wicker proving basket because the dough will pick up the pattern of the weaves. This pattern will become the top of your loaf when you invert the basket on the bakers peel. Remove the basket and slide the loaf into the oven. Wicker proving baskets are also known as "banntons". Use your creativity to make beautiful loaves!

Why Old World Breads

What is the difference between old world and American breads?

Old world breads are traditionally baked without a pan, directly on the oven hearth. The loaves are always formed by hand and they are usually dusted with flour. No two loaves of bread look exactly alike. Europeans favor crusty breads. They savor such with a satisfaction and a contentment that no machine made bread can give. Each loaf is unique in its taste, texture and aroma, almost like if it had its own personality.

The exquisite flavor of old world breads is created by carefully controlled fermentation. In addition, the baking in an adobe brick chamber will impart a delicious savor. This would be lost in metal bread pans as they would inhibit the penetration of the aromatic heat all around the dough.

In the Flanders bread has been baked this way since the dark ages without much change. Nothing can compare with the taste of the characteristic flour dusted old world bread. It has been said that the sliced and wrapped supermarket bread is never touched by human hands, however, only the hands of experience can feel and tell if and when the dough has been kneaded enough. True, the invention of the bread machines has contributed greatly to the incredible growth in home baking, but it cannot be compared with adobe oven baked breads. The taste, smell and the look of such are wonderful to your senses. The crackling sound that the fresh baked bread makes as it comes out the hot adobe oven is beautiful music to your hears. The aroma titillates your nostrils and makes you salivate with the expectation of biting into a nice hot slice slathered with fresh butter. The rough texture of the crust is pleasing to the touch.

Most old world breads rely on just four basic ingredients: flour, salt, water and yeast. Bread in its purest form is crafted from these simple components. This basic formula is the typical everyday bread eaten all over Europe. In medieval times people were generally poor and could not afford the luxury of the white bread enriched with butter and eggs. Such enjoyment was usually reserved for the wealthy or for some very special occasions as weddings, etc. The question often asked is: Why then, do we have such a great variety of old world breads? The answer is: The different methods used to make the dough, the fermentation time and the various ways of adding the yeast. Also, European bakers pay very close attention on how these four basic ingredients affect the fermentation. So, we will examine now these four components and how they can affect the flavor and the texture of the bread with closely controlled fermentation.

The Flour.

The type of mill that grinds the grain has a great effect on the flours performance and flavor. The best flour comes from the stone ground mills. The stone ground process does not overheat the flour and consequently more of the savor is retained.

It is best not to use bleached, bromated or self-rising flour to make old world style breads. The chemical residues that are left behind can interfere with the fermentation process and take away some of the flavor.

Certain special flours called high protein or high gluten should also be avoided. The terms protein and gluten are used synonymously when describing the strength of the flour. Some people find that it is hard to digest anything made from it. This type of flour is produced to make the bread rise a lot higher than normal, yet it is not the best choice if the aim it is to develop the unique old world flavor. European millers utilize some of the continents softer wheat, blending it in with hard wheat, to create a flour with a high level of tolerance or endurance. Endurance is measured by how much fermentation the dough can successfully endure before it begins to break down. The higher the level of endurance the more flavor the baker can develop through controlled fermentation. It is difficult to reproduce an old world bread with high gluten flour. The American product that comes closest to the softer European one is the regular all-purpose unbleached flour. It will not give you the loaf volume, but the flavor will more than compensate for this loss. In the United States if the flour is bleached or if it contains potassium bromate it must be stated on the package. By reading labels, it will not be difficult to avoid such. In a lot of countries on the European continent it is illegal to add chemicals to the flour for possible health hazzards. There good bread has long been appreciated and there seems to be a growing movement in this Country dedicated to finding what was lost: The real staff of life.

The Salt.

Most American cookbooks call for 3 and sometimes 4 teaspoons of salt for every 6 cups of the flour used in the bread dough. Old world recipes usually call for only 1 teaspoon of salt for the same amount. That makes for a big difference. Too much salt does not add flavor, it only disguises it, so that the subtle flavor of the grain is covered and lost.

Some people question the use of salt and swing from one extreme to another, eliminating it altogether from their bread recipes. At an European school for professional bakers we were taught that salt in small amounts is not just an extra ingredient, but it is absolutely necessary to regulate the fermentation, to prevent excessive acidity of the dough, and to strengthen the gluten. It is also a great help in getting a beautiful golden brown crust, where a lot of the savor is concentrated in. Salt also activates different enzymes in the saliva which in turn helps with the proper digestion process. It takes only a very small amount to make a very big change in the flavor of the bread. It is best to pay attention not only to the amount but also to the kind used in your recipes. A natural extra fine salt, without anti-caking agents or other chemicals is the best. The anti-caking agent can interfere with the final rising of the dough. In the Flanders we had available sea salt only, and even up to today I find this the best tasting and the easiest to use.

The Water.

Water also can affect the fermentation and the final flavor of the bread. Extreme hard water tends to slow down the final rising, while very soft water tends to make the dough sticky. The ideal would be somewhere in the middle of the scale of water hardness. Bottled spring water can be an especially good choice if your tap water has chlorine or any other chemicals added to it. If the water in your area is chlorinated another option would be to fill a container with it and let it sit open overnight so as to let the chemical dissipate. Then it can be used to make the bread dough, as chlorine can give an objectionable medicinal flavor to it, and it can also interfere with the final rising.

The Yeast.

Of all the varieties available today, fresh cake or compressed yeast produces a bread with the best flavor. Fresh cake yeast is found in the refrigerated section of the supermarkets and comes in foil-wrapped 0.6 oz. packages with expiration dates. It is best not to purchase or use such past expiration dates. If fresh cake yeast is not easily available in your area, the next best is the active dry, which is a dormant yeast that becomes active when dissolved in liquid.

To develop the unique old world flavor through the longer, cooler and slower Flemish fermentation process it is best to avoid the quick rising yeasts. These are now made in Europe, however, they are not used on most of their own breads. They are made mostly for exportation to the United States.

There are different methods of adding the fresh cake yeast to the dough. The most popular in this Country is commonly called the straight method. The yeast is dissolved into the liquid and then all ingredients are added at once to make the dough.

The most popular method in Europe is what is called the sponge method. In this technique the yeast is dissolved in the liquid with only half of the flour. After this mixture, or sponge, has fermented for about an hour or more, the rest of the flour, and the salt, are added and kneaded into a dough. This will create a superior bread. In the Flanders they add a very small amount, or about ¼ cup for 6 cups of flour, of sourdough to the sponge. This Flemish method became very popular because of the delicious loaves it produced and it has spread all over Europe.

Yeast is a living organism. It is a tiny one cell plant, and like most plants, it doesn't like salt. To accommodate the rough relationship between yeast and salt, always add salt last, after the dough is partly mixed, so that the salt makes only indirect contact with the yeast.

Since the yeast is very sensitive to the heat or to the coolness, always have the flour at room temperature. The liquid to be used for the dough should always be at the temperature indicated in the recipes. The yeast will not work when things are too cold, and too much heat will kill this living organism.

Basic Bread Making Tecniques

Kneading:

After mixing the recipe ingredients in a bowl, turn the dough out onto a lightly floured surface such as a kitchen table or any other smooth top. Flatten the dough and fold it over, toward you. With the heels of your hands push it down forward. Give it a quarter turn and repeat the pushing down forward movement. Repeat the turns and the motions, kneading the dough until it becomes smooth and elastic, usually about 7 minutes.

Rising:

When the dough is smooth and elastic due to the kneading process, return it to the mixing bowl and cover it with a towel. Let the dough rise in a warm(75º F.) draft free place, until doubled in bulk. This may take anywhere from 30 to 90minutes and the timing is usually indicated in the recipes. To see if the dough has risen enough press two finger tips about ½ inch into it. If the impression made by the fingertips springs back, the dough needs a little more time to expand. If the impression stays and does not spring back, the dough is ready for the next step.

Shaping:

The shaping process depends on the type of bread you plan to make. Start by lightly flouring the working surface and your hands. Place the dough on the floured surface.

To make regular loaves, flatten the dough into a rectangular shape with the palm of your hands. Fold the longer sides of the rectangle toward the middle, overlapping about 1 inch. Press the dough flat and roll it tightly to form an oblong loaf. Pinch the seam with your fingers to seal it.

To make round loaves, use both hands to form the dough into round balls. With a slight pressure flatten their bottoms a little unto the working surface.

After you have shaped the dough, place the loaves seam side down onto a generously corn meal dusted bakers peel.

Final Rising:

Having set the loaves onto a corn meal dusted bakers peel, cover them with a towel and let them rise for the time indicated in the recipe. Care should be taken that the dough does not over rise. If this happens, there will be the risk that the loaves will fall inwardly during baking. To correct a dough that has risen too much, quickly reshape it and let it rise again, this time 10 minutes shorter than the time indicated in the recipe. When the loaves are ready to be placed into the oven they need to be treated gently. Avoid bumping or jarring them for this will make them prone to collapse when baking. If you treat them roughly they might turn into door stops instead of bread. The idea is not to turn bread into stones. So, exercise gentleness loading the loaves into the oven. Before doing so, you may want to add some extra finishes.

Finishing Touches:

For a super shine, brush the loaves with an egg wash made by beating one egg with ¼ cup of cold water. For variety, after brushing with the egg wash, sprinkle the loaves with poppy or sesame seeds or with rolled oats.

To give a real old world look, when shaping the loaves roll each one into a little flour. Just before baking slash each top 4 or 5 times diagonally, about ¼ inch deep, for a decorative professional touch. Use a single edge razor with a safety handle or a very sharp knife.

Baking:

It is very important to have the proper oven temperature. An oven that is too hot, or too cool, will adversely affect the quality of the finished product. Most breads are baked between 350°F. and 425°F. Always follow the instructions given in the recipe. A baked loaf should be golden brown.

When the loaves are in the oven for about 15 minutes, open the door and quickly take a peek. If the loaves are browning too quickly, open the rear vent to let some heat escape. Sometimes it may be necessary to leave the door open for a few minutes so that the temperature will drop to the desired degree. A metal thermometer will be very useful for checking the heat. Remember that most of the flavor of the bread is concentrated in the golden brown crust. So, strive to achieve this color. Crowding will make for uneven baking, so try not to overload the oven.

Cooling And Storing:

After the loaves are baked for the appropriate time, open the door and take them out with a bakers peel. Check for doneness by taping the bottom of the loaves with your fingers. If they sound hollow, they are ready. Place them on a wire rack for cooling. If they are placed in a plastic bag they will lose some of the flavor and the crustiness. After slicing and enjoying some, to keep the rest of the loaf fresh, store it cut side down onto a wooden board or into a bread box. A stale loaf can be refreshed by reheating it with a few sprinkles of water. It is important to have a good bread knife that will slice and not tear. Use a good sawing motion with very little pressure. You will not have to worry about storing good bread. It will be eaten quickly and give you a lot of satisfaction. If a loaf doesn't turn out well you can use it to make stuffing, crumbs or croutons, or delicious bread pudding.

Baking Utensils

Bakers peel
Baking sheets
Bowl, glass or ceramic, 1½ to 2 quarts size, for fermentation
Bowls for mixing the dough, 4 quarts size and 6 quarts size
Bowl scraper
Brushes, kitchen type, for egg wash and other bread finishes
Knife, sharp
Measuring cups
Measuring spoons
Oven mittens
Oven thermometer, metal
Rolling pin
Scissors, kitchen type
Spatula
Timer
Whisks
Wire racks for cooling bread
Wooden spoons

Measuring Ingredients

All measures are leveled and based on U.S.A. standards.

For measuring flour, spoon lightly into measuring cup and level off with a straight edge knife or a spatula.

For liquids, set the cup on a flat level surface to check the measuring lines on the side of the cup as it is filled.

A pinch = ⅛ of a teaspoon
3 teaspoons = 1 tablespoon
1 cup liquid = ½ pound
16 tablespoons = 1 cup
1 cup flour = 4 oz.
1 medium egg = 2 oz.
5 medium eggs = 1 cup
6 oz. raisins = 1 cup.

General Oven Temperatures

Very slow..250° F. to 275° F.
Slow..275° F. to 325° F.
Moderate..325° F. to 375° F.
Hot...375° F. to 425° F.
Very hot..425° F. to 475° F.

Bread Baking Temperatures:

Flat Bread..425° F. to 475° F.
Wheat and Rye Breads.............................375° F. to 425° F.
White Bread..350° F. to 375° F.
Sweet and Raisin Breads...........................325° F. to 350° F.

Introduction to Flat Breads

Almost every culture in Europe has a bread it can call its own. Flat breads have been baked on the Continent for countless ages. A crusty round thin bread was found still in the oven in Pompeii, Italy, preserved by the ash from the eruption of Vesuvius in AD 79. This flat bread was about an ½ inch thick and resembled a modern focaccia. It is only in the last few decades that these popular European flat breads are making a showing in the United States.

The name focaccia in Latin means "from the hearth". In Scandinavia "knackebrot" or "platbrood" is traditionally eaten during the long dark winters with smoked herring, cheese or pate. Around the Mediterranean flat bread is often served with olives and olive oil for dipping. Today there is a round thin bread for every mood and taste.

With one firing of your adobe brick oven you can bake a lot of flat breads. It would be perfect for an outdoor pizza party. After you cleaned the ashes out, for the first 30 minutes your oven will be too hot to bake regular loaves, yet it will be just right for the flat breads. This is how they originated. So, have fun exploring the different cultures by experimenting with their wonderfully different types of bread.

Ciabatta

Enjoy this classic Italian flat bread hot, right out the oven. It is delicious when dipped in peppered or savory olive oil or topped with cheese.

2 envelopes (2 tablespoons) of dry yeast.
2 cups warm (110º F.) water
1 teaspoon salt
Approximately 5¾ cups of all purpose unbleached flour

Yield: 4 small loaves.

In a small crock or glass jar dissolve 1 envelope of the dry yeast in 1 cup of the water. Add 1 cup of the flour. Mix well. Let this ferment 24 hours in a warm (75º F.) place.

The next day add all remaining ingredients, working them into a soft dough.

Turn the dough out onto a lightly floured surface and knead for 7 minutes until the dough is smooth. Return the dough to the mixing bowl and cover it with a towel. Let it rise for 1 hour.

Divide the dough into 4 equal pieces. Roll each piece flat with a rolling pin into a 6"x8" rectangle. Dust each with flour.

Place the rectangles onto a bakers peel that has been liberally dusted with corn meal. Prick all over their surfaces with a fork. Let them rise for about 30 minutes.

Bake the ciabattas in a hot adobe oven for about 15 minutes. When they are done, remove them from the oven, let them cool, and enjoy!

Sicilian Flat Bread

This bread puffs out a little when it is baking which will make it real crunchy.

2 envelopes (2 tablespoons) of dry yeast
1 cup warm (110° F.) water
1 cup warm (110° F.) milk
1 tablespoon olive oil
1 teaspoon salt
Approximately 6 cups of all purpose unbleached flour.

Topping:
4 tablespoons olive oil
2 tablespoons dry rosemary leaves, crushed
Dash pepper
¼ teaspoon coarse salt

Yield: 4 small loaves.

In a 6 quart mixing bowl dissolve the dry yeast in the water and the milk. Add 1 cup of the flour. Mix well. Allow this to ferment 1½ hours in a warm (75° F.) place.

Then, add all the remaining ingredients, working them into a dough.

Turn the dough out onto a lightly floured surface and knead for about 7 minutes until the dough is smooth. Return the dough to the mixing bowl and cover it with a towel. Let it rise for 1 hour.

Divide the dough into 4 equal pieces. Roll each piece flat and round with a rolling pin, until it is ¼ inch thick.

Place the loaves onto a bakers peel that has been liberally dusted with corn meal. Brush each piece with a tablespoon of olive oil. Mix the crushed dry rosemary leaves with the coarse salt and the dash of pepper and sprinkle this onto each pieces of dough. Let the dough rise for about 25 minutes.

Bake the loaves in a hot adobe oven for about 12 minutes. Remove them from the oven and enjoy them while warm.

Knakke Brood
Scandinavian Flat Bread

This flat bread has been made in Scandinavia for hundreds of years. It is delicious with smoked cold cuts and cheese.

1 envelope (1 tablespoon) dry yeast
2 cups warm (110° F.) water
1 teaspoon caraway seeds
1 teaspoon dill seeds
½ stick (2 oz.) melted butter
1 teaspoon salt
1 cup rye flour
Approximately 5 cups of all purpose unbleached flour

Yield: 4 small loaves.

In a 6 quart mixing bowl dissolve the dry yeast in the water.

Add all the remaining ingredients, working them into a dough.

Turn the dough out onto a lightly floured surface and knead for about 7 minutes until the dough is smooth. Return the dough to the mixing bowl and cover it with a towel. Let it rise in a warm place until doubled in bulk.

Divide the dough into 4 equal pieces. Sprinkle the work surface with flour, and on it, with a rolling pin, roll each piece until it is flat and round, and about ¼ inch thick.

Dust the loaves with flour and place them onto a bakers peel that has been liberally dusted with corn meal. Prick each loaf all over its top with a fork. Cover the loaves with a towel and let them rise for about 30 minutes.

Bake the loaves in a hot adobe oven for about 12 to 14 minutes. Remove them from the oven and enjoy!

Trappe Brood
Staircase Bread

This bread, called Trappe Brood in the Flanders, is known in Brussels as Fougasse. It goes deliciously well with Italian food. It is crusty and chewy.

2 envelopes (2 tablespoons) of dry yeast
2 cups warm (110° F.) water
¼ cup grated Parmesan cheese to be kneaded into the dough
¼ cup finely chopped onion
¼ cup finely chopped pitted Greek olives
1 teaspoon salt
½ cup whole wheat flour
½ cup rye flour
Approximately 5 cups of all purpose unbleached flour

Topping:
½ cup grated Parmesan cheese
1 teaspoon garlic powder
1 teaspoon rosemary leaves, crushed
Dash ground black pepper
2 tablespoons olive oil for brushing

Yield: 2
In a small ceramic bowl dissolve 1 envelope of dry yeast in ½ cup of the warm water. Add ½ cup of the whole wheat flour. Mix well. Let this ferment for 24 hours.

In the next day add ½ cup of the warm water and ½ cup of the rye flour. Mix it well and let it ferment for 12 hours.

Then add 1 cup of the warm water and 1 envelope of the dry yeast. Place this mixture into a 6 quart mixing bowl and add all the remaining dough ingredients. Work them into a dough.

Turn the dough onto a lightly floured surface and knead it for 7 minutes, or until the dough is smooth.

Return the dough to the mixing bowl and cover it with a towel. Let it rise for about 1 hour.

Divide the dough into 2 equal halves. With a rolling pin, roll each piece flat into a 12"x10" rectangle. Place the rectangles onto a bakers peel that has been liberally dusted with corn meal.

With kitchen scissors make 5 parallel cuts across the dough. Pull by the sides to open the cuts, forming an herringbone pattern or resembling a staircase. Brush each piece with the 1 tablespoon of the olive oil.

Mix the topping ingredients well and sprinkle them onto each rectangle of dough. Let them rise for about 30 minutes.

With the bakers peel insert the breads into the hot adobe oven and bake them for about 12 to 15 minutes. Remove them and enjoy!

Focaccia

This chewy aromatic flat bread is a relative of pizza with a different topping version. It is a good choice for an healthier snack and for entertaining with cheese and wine.

2 envelopes (2 tablespoons) of dry yeast
2 cups warm (110° F.) water
1 egg white (no yolk)
1 tablespoon olive oil
1 teaspoon dried oregano leaves, crushed
1 teaspoon salt
Approximately 6 cups of all purpose unbleached flour

Topping:
½ cup grated Parmesan cheese
1 tablespoon dried rosemary leaves, crushed
1 teaspoon garlic powder
Dash pepper
6 tablespoons of olive oil for brushing

Yield: 2

In a small ceramic bowl dissolve 1 envelope of the dry yeast in ½ cup of the warm water. Add ½ cup of the flour. Mix well. Let this ferment overnight in a warm place.

The next day place this mixture into a 6-quart mixing bowl. Add ½ cup of the flour and the remaining envelope of the yeast. Mix well. Then, add all the remaining dough ingredients and work them into a dough.

Turn the dough out onto a lightly floured surface and knead it for about 7 minutes, until the dough is smooth.

Return the dough to the mixing bowl and cover it with a towel. Let the dough rise in a warm place for about 45 minutes.

Divide the dough into two equal halves. With a rolling pin roll each half into a 12"x 20" rectangle and place them onto a bakers peel that has been liberally dusted with cornmeal. Brush each piece with 3 tablespoons of the olive oil. Dimple the whole surface of each rectangle at 1½ inches intervals by pressing your fingers deep into the oiled dough.

Mix the topping ingredients well and sprinkle them onto both pieces. Let them rise for 30 minutes.

Bake the focaccias in an hot adobe oven for about 12 to 15 minutes. Remove them and enjoy them while warm.

Crusty Pizza

Nothing can compare with a pizza fresh out of a brick adobe oven. This will be a sensation at your outdoor garden party.

2 envelopes (2 tablespoons) of dry yeast
2 cups warm (110º F.) water
1 tablespoon of olive oil
1 egg white (no yolk)
Approximately 6 cups of all purpose unbleached flour

Yield: 2

In a 6-quart mixing bowl dissolve the dry yeast in ½ cup of the warm water. Add all the remaining ingredients, working them into a dough.

Turn the dough out onto a lightly floured surface and knead it for about 7 minutes, until the dough is smooth.

Return the dough to the mixing bowl and cover it with a towel. Let the dough rise in a warm place for about 1 hour.

Divide the dough into two equal halves With a rolling pin roll each half flat into a circle, or into a 12"x10" rectangle, about ¼ inch thick. Set the pieces onto a bakers peel that has been dusted with corn meal. Spread tomato sauce with fresh tomato slices and your favorite topping with cheese on top of each piece. Let them rise for about 25 to 30 minutes.

Bake the pizzas in a hot adobe oven for about 12 to 15 minutes.

NOTE: The key to a delicious pizza is fresh ingredients. Use your imagination for different toppings.

Adobe Oven Old World Bread

Adobe bread of the choicest grain
That ever grows upon the land
Is worthy of all the sweat and pain
To satisfy hunger by your hand

In dark days of war and strife,
The Creators gift for physical life
Baked upon the oven's hearth
The fruit of our living earth.

A poem by Charel Scheele to introduce the next session of recipes for
regular adobe brick oven bread.

Sunflower Loaf

This hearty bread combines the goodness of oats and sunflower seeds for a delicious flavor and it makes for superb toast with a fruit spread.

2 envelopes (2 tablespoons) of dry yeast
2 cups warm (110° F.) milk
½ cup rolled oats
½ cup brown sugar
½ cup hulled sunflower seeds
½ stick (2 oz.) butter, melted
1 egg at room temperature, slightly beaten
1 teaspoon salt
Approximately 5 ½ cups of all purpose unbleached flour

Yield: 2 loaves

In a 6 quart mixing bowl dissolve the dry yeast in the milk. Add the remaining ingredients and work them into a dough.

Turn the dough out onto a lightly floured surface and knead it for about 7 minutes, until the dough is smooth.

Return the dough to the mixing bowl and cover it with a towel. Let it rise until doubled in bulk.

Divide the dough into two equal halves and shape each half into an oblong loaf. Set the loaves onto a bakers peel that has been dusted with corn meal. Cover the loaves with a towel and let them rise for 30 minutes.

Bake the loaves in an adobe oven at 350° F. for about 50 minutes. Remove them with a bakers peel and let them cool.

Crusty Bran Bread

This is a very healthful loaf as no fats or sugar are added. It has a delightful nutty flavor.

1 envelope (1 tablespoon) of dry yeast
2 cups warm (110° F.) water
1 teaspoon salt
1 ½ cups wheat bran
Approximately 4 ½ cups of all purpose unbleached flour

Yield: 2 loaves

In a 6 quart mixing bowl dissolve the yeast in the water. Add the remaining ingredients and work them into a dough.

Turn the dough out onto a lightly floured surface and knead it for about 7 minutes, until the dough is smooth.

Return the dough to the mixing bowl and cover it with a towel. Let the dough rise in a warm place until doubled in bulk.

Divide the dough into two equal halves and shape each half into an oblong loaf. Set the loaves onto a bakers peel that has been dusted with corn meal. Let them rise for about 40 minutes.

Bake the loaves in an adobe oven at 400° F. for about 45 minutes. Remove the loaves from the oven with a bakers peel and enjoy them while warm.

Four Grain Bread

This is a wonderful bread for winter time, very satisfying with a nice bowl of soup.

2 envelopes (2 tablespoons) of dry yeast
2 cups warm (110° F.) water
½ cup whole wheat flour
½ cup rye flour
½ cup rolled oats
½ cup corn meal
1 teaspoon sugar
1 tablespoon corn oil
1 teaspoon salt
Approximately 4 cups of all purpose unbleached flour

Yield: 2 loaves

In a small ceramic bowl dissolve 1 envelope of the dry yeast in ½ cup of the warm water with ½ cup of the whole wheat flour. Let this ferment overnight.

The next day place this mixture into a 6 quart mixing bowl. Add the remaining ingredients and work them into a dough.

Turn the dough out onto a lightly floured surface and knead it for about 7 minutes, until the dough is smooth.

Return the dough to the mixing bowl and cover it with a towel. Let the dough rise in a warm place for about 1 hour.

Divide the dough into two equal halves. Shape the dough into 2 round loaves. Set the loaves onto a bakers peel that has been dusted with corn meal. Let them rise for 30 minutes. With a sharp razor slash across the tops 4 or 5 parallel cuts about ¼ inch deep.

Bake the loaves in an adobe oven at 350° F. for about 1 hour. Remove the loaves from the oven with a bakers peel, and let them cool. Enjoy!

Old Fashioned Bread

A satisfying bread, crusty on the outside yet soft on the inside and delicious with country butter.

2 envelopes (2 tablespoons) of dry yeast
2 cups warm (110° F.) water
1 teaspoon vegetable oil
1 teaspoon salt
½ cup whole wheat flour
Approximately 5 ½ cups of all purpose unbleached flour

Yield: 2 loaves

In a small ceramic bowl dissolve 1 envelope of the dry yeast in ½ cup of the warm water with ½ cup of the whole wheat flour. Let this ferment overnight in a warm place.

The next day pour this fermented mixture into a 6 quart mixing bowl. Add the remaining yeast. Mix well. Let it ferment for about one hour.

Add the remaining ingredients and work them into a dough.

Turn the dough out onto a lightly floured surface and knead it for about 7 minutes, until the dough is smooth.

Return the dough to the mixing bowl and cover it with a towel. Let it rise for one hour.

Divide the dough into two equal halves. Shape them into 2 round loaves. Set the loaves onto a bakers peel that has been dusted with corn meal, and let them rise for 30 minutes. With a razor blade slash 4 or 5 parallel cuts across the tops, about ¼ inch deep.

Bake the loaves in an adobe oven at 400º F. for about 45 minutes. Remove the loaves from the oven with a bakers peel and enjoy them while warm.

Scandinavian Cardamon Rye

This bread has a delightful sweet and spicy savor and it goes real well with a mild cheese.

1 envelope (1 tablespoon) of dry yeast
2 cups warm (110º F.) water
¼ cup light molasses
½ stick (2.oz) butter, melted
½ teaspoon ground cardamon
1 teaspoon salt
1 ½ cups rye flour
Approximately 4 ½ cups of all purpose unbleached flour

Yield: 2 loaves

In a 6 quart mixing bowl dissolve the yeast in the water. Add the remaining ingredients and work them into a dough.

Turn the dough out onto a lightly floured surface and knead it for about 7 minutes, until the dough is smooth.

Return the dough to the mixing bowl and cover it with a towel. Let the dough rise in a warm place for about 1 hour.

Divide the dough into two equal halves and shape each half into an oblong loaf. Set the loaves onto a bakers peel that has been dusted with corn meal. Cover the loaves with a towel and let them rise for 30 minutes.

With a razor blade slash 4 or 5 times diagonally across the top of the loaves about ¼ inch deep.

Bake the loaves in an adobe oven at 375º F. for about 45 minutes. Remove the loaves from the oven, with a bakers peel, and enjoy them while warm.

Onion Cheese Rye

The combination of onion and cheese in this rye bread will give it an exquisite flavor that will make it a wonderful accompaniment to smoked meats and beer.

1 envelope (1 tablespoon) of dry yeast
2 cups warm (110° F.) water
1 tablespoon vegetable oil
1 small onion, finely chopped
¾ cup shredded cheddar cheese
1 teaspoon salt
1 cup rye flour
Approximately 5 cups of all purpose unbleached flour

Yield: 2 loaves

In a 6 quart mixing bowl dissolve the yeast in the water. Add the remaining ingredients and work them into a dough.

Turn the dough out onto a lightly floured surface and knead it for about 7 minutes, until the dough is smooth.

Return the dough to the mixing bowl and cover it with a towel. Let the dough rise in a warm place for about one hour.

Divide the dough into two equal halves and shape each half into a round loaf. Set the loaves onto a bakers peel that has been dusted with corn meal. Cover them with a towel and let them rise for 40 minutes.

With a razor blade make 4 or 5 diagonal slashes about ¼ inch deep across the top of the loaves.

Bake the loaves in an adobe oven at 400° F. for about 40 minutes.

Remove the loaves from the oven with a bakers peel. Enjoy!

Nordic Farm Bread

This is a hearty country bread, delicious for sandwiches, yet also very good with butter and jam.

2 envelopes (2 tablespoons) of dry yeast
2 cups warm (110° F.) milk
1 stick (4 oz.) butter, melted
½ cup brown sugar
1 egg at room temperature, slightly beaten
1 teaspoon salt
1 ½ cups whole wheat flour
Approximately 4½ cups of all purpose unbleached flour

Yield: 2 loaves

In a 6 quart mixing bowl dissolve the yeast in the milk. Mix well. Add the remaining ingredients and work them into a dough.

Turn the dough out onto a lightly floured surface and knead it for about 7 minutes, until the dough is smooth.

Return the dough to the mixing bowl and cover it with a towel. Let the dough rise in a warm place for one hour.

Divide the dough into two equal halves, and shape each half into an oblong loaf. Set the loaves onto a bakers peel that has been dusted with corn meal. Cover them with a towel and let them rise 40 minutes.

With a razor blade make 4 or 5 diagonal slashes about ¼ inch deep across the top of the loaves.

Bake the loaves in an adobe oven at 375° F. for about one hour. Remove the bread from the oven. Enjoy!

Normal Bread

After I had baked a lot of whole grain breads my niece, Irvi, asked me: "Uncle, why don't you bake normal bread for a change?". She was referring to the white supermarket product that for so many children looks like the accepted standard. So I have included this recipe for a soft white loaf to please all youngsters who want "normal" bread.

2 envelopes (2 tablespoons) of dry yeast
2 cups warm (110º F.) milk
½ stick (2oz.) butter, melted
½ cup sugar
1 teaspoon salt
Approximately 6 cups of all purpose unbleached flour

Yield: 2 loaves

In a 6 quart mixing bowl dissolve the yeast in the milk. Add the remaining ingredients and work them into a dough.

Turn the dough out onto a lightly floured surface and knead it for about 7 minutes, until the dough is smooth.

Return the dough to the mixing bowl and cover it with a towel. Let the dough rise in a warm place for about 1 hour.

Divide the dough into two equal halves and shape each half into a loaf that fits a bread pan that has been lightly greased with a vegetable oil. Cover the loaves with a towel and let them rise for 40 minutes.

Load the bread pans into the adobe oven when its temperature hovers from 350° F. to 360° F. and let them bake for one hour. When ready, using long oven mitts or a bakers peel, unload the pans. After removing the loaves from the pans, let them cool, and—voila—you have "normal" bread.

NOTE: This bread will burn easy. Make sure that the internal temperature of your oven is around 350° F.. If your oven is too hot, open the back flue to cool it down. Close the vent and you will be ready to bake at the desired degrees.

Cinnamon Raisin Swirl

A deliciously sweet bread that is a success with children and adults alike.

2 envelopes (2 tablespoons) of dry yeast.
2 cups warm (110º F.) water.
½ stick (2 oz.) butter, melted
½ cup brown sugar
2 eggs at room temperature, slightly beaten
1 cup raisins
1 teaspoon salt
Approximately 6 cups of all purpose unbleached flour

Filling:
½ stick (2 oz.) butter, melted, for brushing.
½ cup brown sugar
1 teaspoon ground cinnamon

Yield: 1 large loaf

In a 6 quart mixing bowl dissolve the yeast in the milk. Add the remaining bread ingredients and work them into a dough.

Turn the dough out onto a lightly floured surface and knead it for about 7 minutes, until the dough is smooth.

Return the dough to the mixing bowl and cover it with a towel. Let the dough rise in a warm place for about 1 hour.

With a rolling pin, roll the dough out into a 20" x 10" rectangle. Brush the top with the melted butter from the filling ingredients. From the same, combine the brown sugar and the cinnamon and mix them well. Sprinkle this mixture over the rectangle. Starting at the narrow end roll the dough just like you would a jelly roll. Set the loaf seam side down onto a lightly greased baking sheet, and cover it with a towel. Let the dough rise for 45 minutes.

Slide the baking sheet with the loaf into the adobe oven that has an internal temperature of 350° F. and let it bake for about 1 hour.

Note: This bread burns easily. Make sure that the temperature of your oven is 350° F.

Raisin Bread

This sweet and spicy bread is a winner for a coffee break or as a dessert with honey or jam.

2 envelopes (2 tablespoons) of dry yeast.
2 cups warm (110° F.) milk
½ stick (2 oz.) butter, melted
½ cup sugar
1 egg at room temperature, slightly beaten
Grated rind of 1 lemon
1 cup raisins
1 teaspoon salt
Approximately 6 cups of all purpose unbleached flour

Yield: 2 loaves

In a 6 quart mixing bowl dissolve 1 envelope of the yeast into 1 cup of the milk. Add 1 cup of the flour. Mix well. Let this ferment for about one hour.

Then add the other envelope of the yeast and the other cup of the milk. Mix well. Add the remaining ingredients and work them into a dough.

Turn the dough out onto a lightly floured surface and knead it for about 7 minutes, until the dough is smooth.

Return the dough to the mixing bowl and cover it with a towel. Let the dough rise in a warm place for about 1 hour.

Divide the dough into two equal halves and shape each half into an oblong loaf. Set the loaves onto a baking sheet that has been lightly greased with a vegetable oil. Cover the loaves with a towel and let them rise again for 45 minutes.

Bake the loaves in an adobe oven at 350° F. for about 1 hour. Remove the loaves from the oven with a bakers peel and let them cool down. Enjoy!

Introduction to Sourdough Starter

To begin with, let's take out the mystery out of the sourdough starter.

You probably have heard that some sourdough cultures are anywhere from 100 to 150 years old. However, the flavor and the smell of a sourdough starter is not created by age.

The flavor and the aroma originate from the first ten days it takes to start a culture. Once the starter is fully ripe and mature it will change very little over the time. It would take many years to change its fragrance and savor. Most of the fluctuations will happen at the beginning, and especially so if you leave the starter container uncovered during the first ten days. Leaving the fermentation process exposed will attract wild yeast cells that abide in the surrounding environment. These play a role in determining the acidity and the consequent aroma.

Another factor that plays a role is what it is used to start the process. It makes a big difference if potato cooking water was used, if sugar was added, and what kind of yeast was employed. The quantities of each item will also affect the end result. These are just some of the factors involved. Timing and the temperature also influence the maturation of the wild yeast cells. If the starting fermentation is too quick and if you didn't wait long enough for it to reach ripeness and maturity, your finished product will be affected.

In the Flanders every baker had his own theory and formula on how to have the perfect sourdough starter. Their formulas were guarded with great secrecy, and especially so if their bread was very popular. This secrecy added perhaps to the air of mystery that surrounds sourdough starters.

The biggest secret to making a good sourdough is patience and perseverance. It is good to experiment with different ways so as to find what your preference is. Your individual taste is what counts. You might want to try with different liquids, such as plain water, potato or other vegetable cooking water, or even beer. You may increase or decrease the amount of yeast and or sugar. All of these will change the flavor and the fragrance of the starter.

The purpose of using the sugar at the beginning is not to sweeten the starter, just to feed the yeast cells. The microscopic one celled yeast plants are alive and they are able to break down the carbohydrates into alcohol and carbon dioxide. Bakers use yeast for the carbon dioxide that forms the bubbles and make the dough rise. As the alcohol permeates the dough it creates the flavor and the texture you desire. The alcohol evaporates in the baking process leaving behind a rich delicious savor.

It is not essential to add sugar to the starter. The yeast cells can feed on the natural sugars found in the flour. Sourdough starter made without sugar ferments much slower and it usually turns out a much milder flavor that is more preferred on the other side of the Atlantic. For many it makes a more delicious bread. So, patience is required. Let it ferment slowly until it is totally ripe. I will give you my favorite recipe. After trying it, you might want to make your own changes and experiments. Each change you make will affect the smell and the flavor. The variety will be endless. Each starter has its own behavioral characteristics. Some are very pungent and sour, others are much milder. The yeast cells will react differently with each type of flour.

These are some pointers in making a good sourdough starter: First, do not use bleached flour. The residues of the bleaching agents used often make for a bitter taste in the starter. Second, do not use a metal utensil such as a spoon, a fork or a mixing bowl. The chemical reactions between the metal and the acid in the starter will impart a bad flavor to the batch. Third, remember that extreme heat will kill the starter.

If the starter is fully mature, and yet, you do no want to use it right away, it should be stored in the refrigerator. The cold will make it dormant, however, it will not kill it. The day before you plan to make your sourdough bread retrieve the starter from the refrigerator, and let it slowly come to the room temperature. A cold starter will not make the dough rise. You may notice that some liquid has formed on the surface. Beat it vigorously with a wooden spoon so as to incorporate the liquid in the batter. When the starter has reached the room temperature, pour out what you need and replenish the amount leftover by adding 1 cup of unbleached flour and 1 cup of tepid (100° F.) water. Mix well with a wooden spoon and let it ferment for 24 hours at the room temperature. Afterwards, you can store the starter in the refrigerator again. In this way, you can keep it alive for years. If the starter is not used for 2 weeks, pour out 1 cup of it and replenish it again using the formula above. This will keep it alive, healthy and bubbly.

There is a school of thought among professional European bakers that contend that only the fresh compressed cake yeast will give a good flavor to a sourdough starter. They insist strictly on fresh yeast. It really is the best. However if in some areas it is very difficult to obtain it, you may use the dry yeast. I use it in my bread recipes but not for sourdough starters. Just do not use the quick rising yeast. It takes time, not speed, for the real rich flavor to develop. The fresh yeast is mostly found in the dairy or refrigerated areas of the supermarkets. Make sure that the yeast is fresh and not past the expiration dates. If your starter begins to mold or discolor throw it away. It has either attracted a bad strain of wild yeast cells or the cake yeast you used was past the expiration date. This usually doesn't happen very often. The starter should have a pleasing sour smell and a somewhat yeasty aroma that is pleasing to the nostrils. It should have the consistency of a cake batter and a crisp light cream color. With patience an ingenuity you will attain the desired results.

Making the Starter

The success in making a flavorful starter is dependent mostly upon providing the best environment for the right yeast cells. Not all yeast cells are the same. To attract and cultivate the right kind that will produce the best and the most flavor, start with a draft free and somewhat cool place with a temperature between 65° and 68° F.. This temperature range will make for a slow and steady fermentation, and it is also the best for the particular yeast cells that are desirable to produce the best flavor and that thrive in a cooler environment. A starter made in such an atmosphere will be deliciously acidic but not too pungent or bitter, and it will have enough strength to rise the dough.

In a warmer place the starter will ferment faster and save time but it will not develop the unique old world flavor. If you want a good sourdough starter you cannot shorten the fermentation timetable.

Mix the following ingredients in a scrupulously clean ceramic or glass bowl with a scrupulously clean wooden spoon:

> 1 cup tepid (100° F.) potato cooking water
> 1 cup unbleached all purpose flour
> ¼ cake fresh compressed yeast
> ¼ teaspoon sugar

Dissolve the fresh yeast into the potato cooking water. Add the sugar and the flour. Mix well.

Let this mixture ferment in a somewhat cool place (65° -68° F.) for 5 days (120 hours). Keep the ceramic bowl uncovered to attract some of the wild yeast cells of the surrounding environment These will add an unique and interesting personality to your starter.

Stir this mixture twice a day, with a scrupulously clean wooden spoon, to incorporate into the batter any crust that has formed on the top.

After 5 days (120 hours) add 1 cup of unbleached all purpose flour and 1 cup of tepid (100° F.) bottled water. Mix this thoroughly with a clean wooden spoon. Let it ferment again for 5 days (120 hours).

The starter is ready now for use, or to be stored in the refrigerator.

Introduction to Sourdough Breads

Welcome to the international savor adventure of old world sourdough breads. As you start baking sourdough breads in your adobe and brick oven, a whole new world of delicious flavors is opened to you. Your taste-bud will travel from Western to Eastern Europe, stopping in Belgium, Holland and Germany to name just a few of the places visited.

Old world sourdough bread is all about going back to simpler ways of baking that existed way before the giant bread factories changed our eating habits.

Amazingly, baking sourdoughs do not require sleepless nights or slaving long hours in the kitchen. The key is a little bit of forethought and planning. This is not such a difficult task. The ingredient mostly needed is patience. Expensive equipment is not required. In the next recipes you may add a ½ cake of fresh compressed yeast to shorten fermentation, however what you gain in time you will lose in flavor.

In the following section I've compiled some recipes with the unique taste of the old Continent, and I have endeavored to share basic baking instructions and ideas. May you embark on your trip of discovery and enjoy a new world of flavors from the old world.

East European Sourdough Rye

This classic rye bread recipe came from the Balkans and it is deliciously satisfying with just plain butter, or a slice of Monterey cheese.

1 cup of sourdough starter at room temperature. (see recipe for starter)
1 cup warm (110° F.) water
2 tablespoons caraway seeds
1 teaspoon salt
½ cup rye flour
Approximately 4¼ cups of all purpose unbleached flour

Yield: 2 loaves.

Mix all the ingredients in a 6 quart mixing bowl and work them into a dough.

Turn the dough out onto a lightly floured surface and knead it for about 7 minutes, until the dough is smooth.

Return the dough to the mixing bowl and cover it with a towel. Let the dough rise in a warm place for about 2 to 2½ hours.

Divide the dough into two equal halves and shape each half into an oblong loaf.

Set the loaves onto a bakers peel that has been dusted with corn meal. Cover them with a towel and let them rise again for 2 hours.

With a razor blade make 4 or 5 diagonal slashes about ¼ inch deep across the top of the loaves, and slide them onto the hot oven hearth.

Bake the loaves at 400° F. for 50 minutes. Remove them from the oven an let them cool.

Swedish Sourdough Farm Bread

This compact loaf has a delectable taste and as a bonus it will stay fresh for days.

1 cup of sourdough starter at room temperature.(see recipe for starter)
1 cup warm (110º F.) water
1 tablespoon molasses
½ stick (2 oz.) butter, melted
1 teaspoon salt
1 cup rye flour
2 cups whole wheat flour
Approximately 2¾ cups of all purpose unbleached flour

Yield: 2 loaves.

Mix all the ingredients in a 6 quart mixing bowl and work them into a dough.

Turn the dough out onto a lightly floured surface and knead it for about 7 minutes, until the dough is smooth.

Return the dough to the mixing bowl and cover it with a towel. Let the dough rise in a warm place for about 2 to 2½ hours.

Divide the dough into two equal halves and shape each half into an oblong loaf.

Set the loaves onto a bakers peel that has been dusted with corn meal. Cover them with a towel and let them rise again for 2 hours.

With a razor blade make 4 or 5 diagonal slashes about ¼ inch deep across the top of the loaves and slide them onto the hot oven hearth.

Bake the loaves at 400° F. for 50 minutes. Remove them from the oven an let them cool. Enjoy!

Sourdough Black Bread

To make it black some bakers have added caramelized sugar, chocolate, coffee, or other additives in their recipes. Commercialized loaves have the addition of artificial colors. This is not a really dark colored bread. It is a simple yet very tasty recipe that will make for a traditional heavy loaf. Thinly slice it and serve it with European cold cuts. Just delicious!

1 cup of sourdough starter at room temperature.(see recipe for starter)
1 cup warm (110° F.) water.
¼ cup dark molasses
1 teaspoon salt
2 cups dark rye flour
Approximately 3¾ cups of all purpose unbleached flour

Yield: 2 loaves.

Mix all the ingredients in a 6 quart mixing bowl and work them into a dough.

Turn the dough out onto a lightly floured surface and knead it for about 7 minutes, until the dough is smooth.

Return the dough to the mixing bowl and cover it with a towel. Let the dough rise in a warm place for about 2 to 2½ hours.

Divide the dough into two equal halves and shape each half into an oblong loaf.

Set the loaves onto a bakers peel that has been dusted with corn meal. Cover them with a towel and let them rise again for 2 hours.

With a razor blade make 4 or 5 diagonal slashes about ¼ inch deep across the top of the loaves and slide them onto the hot oven hearth.

Bake the loaves at 400° F. for 50 minutes. Remove them from the oven an let them cool. Enjoy!

Sourdough Rye with Currants

A sweet sourdough bread that, served with fruit spreads, is an excellent choice for a tea party.

1 cup of sourdough starter at room temperature.(see recipe for starter)
1 cup warm (110° F.) water.
1 cup currants
¼ cup brown sugar
½ stick (2 oz.) butter, melted
Pinch cinnamon
1 teaspoon salt
1 cup rye flour
Approximately 4¾ cups of all purpose unbleached flour

Yield: 2 loaves.

Mix all the ingredients in a 6 quart mixing bowl and work them into a dough.

Turn the dough out onto a lightly floured surface and knead it for about 7 minutes, until the dough is smooth.

Return the dough to the mixing bowl and cover it with a towel. Let the dough rise in a warm place for about 2 to 2½ hours.

Divide the dough into two equal halves and shape each half into an oblong loaf.

Set the loaves onto a bakers peel that has been dusted with corn meal. Cover them with a towel and let them rise again for 2 hours.

With a razor blade make 4 or 5 diagonal slashes about ¼ inch deep across the top of the loaves and slide them onto the hot oven hearth.

Bake the loaves at 400° F. for 50 minutes. Remove them from the oven an let them cool. Enjoy!

Pain au Levain Blanc

This French levain (sourdough) white bread has a nice crust, a chewy texture and a delicious flavor. It is amazing that such few ingredients make for such wonderfully tasty loaves!

1 cup of sourdough starter at room temperature.(see recipe for starter)
1 cup warm (110° F.) water
1 teaspoon salt
Approximately 5¾ cups of all purpose unbleached flour

Yield: 2 loaves.

Mix all the ingredients in a 6 quart mixing bowl and work them into a dough.

Turn the dough out onto a lightly floured surface and knead it for about 7 minutes, until the dough is smooth.

Return the dough to the mixing bowl and cover it with a towel. Let the dough rise in a warm place for about 2 to 2½ hours.

Divide the dough into two equal halves and shape each half into a long loaf.

Set the loaves onto a bakers peel that has been dusted with corn meal. Cover them with a towel and let them rise again for 2 hours.

With a razor blade make 4 or 5 diagonal slashes about ¼ inch deep across the top of the loaves and slide them into the hot oven.

Bake the loaves at 410° F. to 420° F. for 45 minutes. Remove them from the oven an let them cool. Enjoy!

Country Pain au Levain

This country version of the French sourdough bread is so delicious that you will not think of its healthy benefits and also that is non-fattening.

1 cup of sourdough starter at room temperature.(see recipe for starter)
1 cup warm (110° F.) water
1 teaspoon salt
½ cup rye flour
½ cup whole wheat flour
Approximately 4¾ cups of all purpose unbleached flour

Yield: 2 loaves.

Mix all the ingredients in a 6 quart mixing bowl and work them into a dough.

Turn the dough out onto a lightly floured surface and knead it for about 7 minutes, until the dough is smooth.

Return the dough to the mixing bowl and cover it with a towel. Let the dough rise in a warm place for about 2 to 2½ hours.

Divide the dough into two equal halves and shape each half into an long loaf.

Set the loaves onto a bakers peel that has been dusted with corn meal. Cover them with a towel and let them rise again for 2 hours.

With a razor blade make 4 or 5 diagonal slashes about ¼ inch deep across the top of the loaves and slide them into the hot oven.

Bake the loaves at 410° F. to 420° F. for 40 minutes. Remove them from the oven an let them cool. Enjoy!

Sourdough Wheat Bread

This is a hearty and grainy bread, full flavored and non-fattening. What more can you ask for?

1 cup of sourdough starter at room temperature.(see recipe for starter)
1 cup warm (110° F.) water
1 teaspoon salt
3 cups whole wheat flour
Approximately 2¾ cups of all purpose unbleached flour

Yield: 2 loaves.

Mix all the ingredients in a 6 quart mixing bowl and work them into a dough.

Turn the dough out onto a lightly floured surface and knead it for about 7 minutes, until the dough is smooth.

Return the dough to the mixing bowl and cover it with a towel. Let the dough rise in a warm place for about 2 to 2½ hours.

Divide the dough into two equal halves and shape each half into an oblong loaf.

Set the loaves onto a bakers peel that has been dusted with corn meal. Cover them with a towel and let them rise again for 2 hours.

With a razor blade make 4 or 5 diagonal slashes about ¼ inch deep across the top of the loaves and slide them onto the hot oven hearth.

Bake the loaves at 410° F. to 420° for 40 minutes. Remove them from the oven an let them cool. Enjoy!

Introduction to Small Breads

By skillfully managing the dough, an endless variety of small breads can be made such as, rolls of all shapes and sizes, bread sticks, etc. It all depends on your creativity and ingenuity. As an example, when you divide the dough into two equal halves, one half can be made into a regular loaf while the other half can be shaped into one dozen rolls.

Round rolls are very simple to make. After dividing your dough into equal roll size pieces, flour your hands and manually form each piece into a ball, pressing it lightly to the work surface so as to flatten the bottom. Place the rolls 1½ inches apart onto a corn meal dusted baking sheet.

For bread sticks flour an evenly smooth surface, and your hands, then, roll each separate piece of the dough with your palms to form a pencil thin rope usually about 9 inches long. You may leave the sticks long, coil them like snakes, twist them into spirals resembling snails or close the ends together, resembling rings.

It is fun to experiment with shaping the rolls any way you wish. For added variety, after brushing with an egg wash, sprinkle each one with sesame, poppy or other edible seeds.

Since small breads require less heat, bake the regular loaves first. After your adobe oven's temperature has come down a little you can load it with the rolls.

Any recipe in this book can be doubled if the need may be.

Rolls are a favorite for outdoor barbecues and picnics and the aroma of them baking in your backyard will add to the atmosphere. Your adobe and brick oven will quickly become the center of attraction and a real conversation piece.

Sour Cream Soft Bread Sticks

Popular in Europe, these soft and pleasing bread sticks make a nice addition to soup or stew.

2 envelopes (2 tablespoons) of dry yeast.
2 cups warm (110° F.) milk
2 tablespoons sugar
3 eggs, at room temperature, lightly beaten
½ cup sour cream
Grated rind of 1 large size lemon
1¼ teaspoon salt
Approximately 6½ cups of all purpose unbleached flour

Yield: 24 bread sticks.

In a 6 quart mixing bowl dissolve the yeast in the milk. Add the remaining ingredients and work them into a dough.

Turn the dough out onto a lightly floured surface and knead it for about 7 minutes, until the dough is smooth.

Return the dough to the mixing bowl and cover it with a towel. Let the dough rise in a warm place for about 45 minutes.

Divide the dough into 24 equal size pieces and shape each piece into a pencil thin rope about 9 inches long.

Set the sticks of dough about 1½ inches apart onto a baking sheet that has been liberally dusted with corn meal. Cover them with a towel and let them rise for 25 minutes.

Bake them in an adobe oven at 375° F. for about 22 minutes or until golden brown. Remove the bread sticks from the oven and serve them warm.

Crusty Hard Rolls

These crusty rolls taste like French bread and they are delicious with butter, for dinner.

2 envelopes (2 tablespoons) of dry yeast
2 cups warm (110° F.) water
½ stick (2 oz.) soft butter
3 egg whites, at room temperature
1¼ teaspoon salt
Approximately 6¼ cups of all purpose unbleached flour

Yield: 24 rolls.

In a 6 quart mixing bowl dissolve 1 envelope of the dry yeast in 1 cup of the warm water. Add 1 cup of the flour. Mix well. Let this ferment for 3½ hours.

Then, add the rest of the yeast and the water. Mix well. Add the remaining ingredients and work them into a dough.

Turn the dough out onto a lightly floured surface and knead it for about 7 minutes, until the dough is smooth.

Return the dough to the mixing bowl and cover it with a towel. Let it rise for 45 minutes.

Divide the dough into 24 equal-size pieces and shape each piece into a round roll.

Set the rolls about 1½ inches apart onto a baking sheet that has been liberally dusted with corn meal. Cover them with a towel and let them rise for 25 minutes.

Bake the rolls in an adobe oven at 375° F. for about 22 minutes or until golden brown. Remove them from the oven and let them cool.

Soft Potato Rolls

These rolls are soft, rich tasting, and they will stay fresh for several days.

2 envelopes (2 tablespoons) of dry yeast
2 cups warm (110° F.) milk
1 stick (4 oz.) soft butter
½ cup sugar
2 eggs, at room temperature, lightly beaten
½ cup dry potato flakes
1 teaspoon salt
Approximately 6 cups of all purpose unbleached flour

Yield: 24 rolls.

In a 6 quart mixing bowl dissolve the yeast in the milk. Add the remaining ingredients and work them into a dough.

Turn the dough out onto a lightly floured surface and knead it for about 7 minutes, until the dough is smooth.

Return the dough to the mixing bowl and cover it with a towel. Let the dough rise in a warm place for about 45 minutes.

Divide the dough into 24 equal size pieces and shape each piece into a round roll.

Set the rolls about 1½ inches apart onto a baking sheet that has been dusted with corn meal. Cover them with a towel and let them rise for 25 minutes.

Bake the rolls in an adobe oven at 375° F. for about 22 minutes or until golden brown. Remove them from the oven and enjoy!

Fat free Bran Rolls

These healthy rolls have a delicious nutty flavor due to the bran. Since they do not keep well, serve them right away. They are so good you will not have a problem with storing them.

2 envelopes (2 tablespoons) of dry yeast
2 cups warm (110° F.) water
1 cup raw millers bran
1 teaspoon salt
Approximately 5 cups of all purpose unbleached flour

Yield: 24 rolls

In a 6 quart mixing bowl dissolve the yeast in the water. Add the remaining ingredients and work them into a dough.

Turn the dough out onto a lightly floured surface and knead it for about 7 minutes, until the dough is smooth.

Return the dough to the mixing bowl and cover it with a towel. Let the dough rise in a warm place for about 45 minutes.

Divide the dough into 24 equal size pieces and shape each piece into a round roll.

Set the rolls about 1½ inches apart onto a baking sheet that has been dusted with corn meal. Cover them with a towel and let them rise for 25 minutes.

Bake the rolls in an adobe oven at 400° F. for about 20 minutes or until golden brown. Remove them from the oven and enjoy!

Bulgarian Rolls

Rich tasting, with a delectable tangy flavor, these rolls are a wonderful accompaniment for lunch and dinner, yet they also stand out on their own just with butter, cheese or cold cuts.

2 envelopes (2 tablespoons) of dry yeast
2 cups warm (110° F.) buttermilk
1 tablespoon sour cream
2 tablespoons soft butter
1 teaspoon caraway seeds
1 teaspoon salt
½ cup rye flour
Approximately 5½ cups of all purpose unbleached flour

Yield: 24 rolls.

In a 6 quart mixing bowl dissolve the yeast in the buttermilk. Add the remaining ingredients and work them into a dough.

Turn the dough out onto a lightly floured surface and knead it for about 7 minutes, until the dough is smooth.

Return the dough to the mixing bowl and cover it with a towel. Let the dough rise in a warm place for about 45 minutes.

Divide the dough into 24 equal size pieces and shape each piece into a round roll.

Set the rolls about 1½ inches apart onto a baking sheet that has been dusted with corn meal. Cover them with a towel and let them rise for 25 minutes.

Bake the rolls in an adobe oven at 375º F. for about 22 minutes or until golden brown. Remove them from the oven, let them cool and enjoy!

Multi-Grain Rolls

These hearty rolls stand out on their own in flavor and are just wonderful with smoked meats, cheese and Dutch beer.

2 envelopes (2 tablespoons) of dry yeast
2 cups warm (110° F.) water
1 tablespoon vegetable oil
1 tablespoon sugar
½ cup rolled oats
½ cup rye flour
½ cup corn meal
½ cup raw millers bran
1 teaspoon salt
Approximately 4 cups of all purpose unbleached flour

Yield: 24 rolls.

In a 6 quart mixing bowl dissolve the yeast in the water. Add the remaining ingredients and work them into a dough.

Turn the dough out onto a lightly floured surface and knead it for about 7 minutes, until the dough is smooth.

Return the dough to the mixing bowl and cover it with a towel. Let the dough rise in a warm place for about 45 minutes.

Divide the dough into 24 equal size pieces and shape each piece into a round roll.

Set the rolls about 1½ inches apart onto a baking sheet that has been dusted with corn meal. Cover them with a towel and let them rise for 25 minutes.

Bake the rolls in an adobe oven at 375º F. for about 22 minutes or until golden brown. Remove them from the oven, let then cool and enjoy!

Baking Problems and Solutions That Work

I am very thankful and appreciative for the opportunity to share my baking knowledge and experience with you. As with any human effort at times things go wrong and do not turn out the way we expect. When this happens, it is time to pause and look back to see what went wrong in order to learn and not to repeat the error. This knowledge will help you to improve your baking skills and your proficiency.

To help you get started in your adobe brick oven baking adventure I wrote some of the best recipes, however, do not hold back from trying your own formulas and from experimenting on your favorite ideas. Baking is really a learning experience repeated in every loaf. I hope the information in this book will put you on a long and pleasant road of bread baking. So, do not give up if things go wrong. Remember what I mentioned before:—if your loaf doesn't turn out the way you wanted it to, you can always make croutons, stuffing, and/or delicious bread pudding with it.

Following, you will find some suggestions to help you avoid the most common mistakes that can occur in bread baking:

Oven Too Hot:
1) Crust too dark
2) Small loaves
3) Center is sticky

Oven Too Cool:
1) Crust too light
2) Large loaves
3) Center dry

Bread Collapses in Oven:
1) Dough was over proofed
2) Loaves were handled roughly before loaded into the oven
3) Dough was not kneaded long enough

No Volume:
1) Old yeast
2) Not enough yeast
3) Under proofed

Too Much Volume:
1) Too much yeast
2) Over proofed
3) Oven too cool

Slow Rising:
1) Cold dough
2) Old yeast
3) Not enough yeast

Fast Rising:
1) Dough too warm
2) Too much yeast
3) No salt added

Fermentation Time Too Short:
1) Poor oven spring
2) Blistered top crust
3) Holes inside loaf

Fermentation Time Too Long:
1) No yeast activity
2) No oven spring
3) Bread falls in the oven

Bread Rips and Tears in Oven:
1) Dough was under proofed
2) Dough stood in a drafty place
3) Seam of loaf placed on top

Crust Too Hard:
1) Oven too hot
2) Baked too long
3) Dough too stiff

Bread Sticky in the Middle:
1) Oven too cool
2) Not baked long enough
3) Under proofed

Uneven Rising:
1) Dough shaped incorrectly
2) Oven was over crowded
3) Dough left in a drafty place

Loaves Spread Out:
1) Dough was too soft
2) Loaves were not rolled tightly enough
3) Not enough flour was used

Loaves Not Baked Even:
1) Coals were not spread evenly on oven hearth
2) Oven door not closed securely or tightly
3) Flue or vent hole left partly open

Top Crust Too Dark:
1) Too much egg wash
2) Oven too hot
3) Too much sugar

Very Thick Crust:
!) Oven not hot enough
2) Dough stood in a drafty place
3) Over proofing

Sourdough Starter Has Bad Taste:
1) Chlorinated water was used to replenish it
2) Bleached flour was used to replenish it
3) Starter was stirred with a metal utensil

Bread Gets Stale Fast:
1) Cut side not turned onto bread board on storing
2) Placed in plastic bag while still warm
3) It was left sitting out in a drafty place

Big Holes In Crumb:
1) Wrong kind of flour (ex. pastry flour) was used
2) Liquid was too warm
3) Too much flour used for molding

Dough Is Stiff and Hard To Handle:
1) Flour or water were not rightly measured
2) Not enough time to ferment properly
3) Eggs or butter called for in recipe were not added

Dough Is Too Sticky To Handle:
1) It was not kneaded long enough
2) Wrong kind of flour was used (i.e. pastry or cake flour)
3) Flour or water were not rightly measured.

About the Author

Charel Scheele descended from a long line of bakers, as it was customary in Europe to pass along the father's profession to the sons. One of the family's bakeries was in the Dutch part of the Flanders where he grew up. Helping out in the bakery since he was a child, as the years went by, he became acquainted and experienced with all the aspects of baking, running the business and the baked goods store.

After graduating from High school he graduated from two different European schools for professional bakers and successfully completed courses in business administration.

He traveled extensively and built adobe-mud and brick ovens in Europe, Brazil and in the United States.

Presently he lives in the northern mountains of New Mexico and he has two adobe ovens that he built in his back yard. He uses them often to bake bread and pizza.

Charel has written several books on the art of making old world breads, and he considers himself addicted to good European style bread.

In this book he highlights the rewarding aspects of bread baking in the old fashion way and the enjoyment one can derive from it. For him it is a great adventure and he would like others to share in it. His step-by-step directions are easy to follow and even first-timers and amateurs can learn and enjoy making and using an adobe style oven.

While there may not be a consensus on which type of bread tastes best, it is safe to say that adobe oven bread ranks among the most flavorful. These free-form hand crafted breads are outstanding, crusty on the outside, soft on the inside and Charel Scheele is convinced that once they are tried out, many will be addicted like he is to their wonderful savor. He also believes that a bread revolution has happened in the United States with some marvelous results and far-reaching consequences. He hopes you will be a part of it too. Better bread for better health!

Index

0-595-24342-8